SUPERBASE 8

FALLON

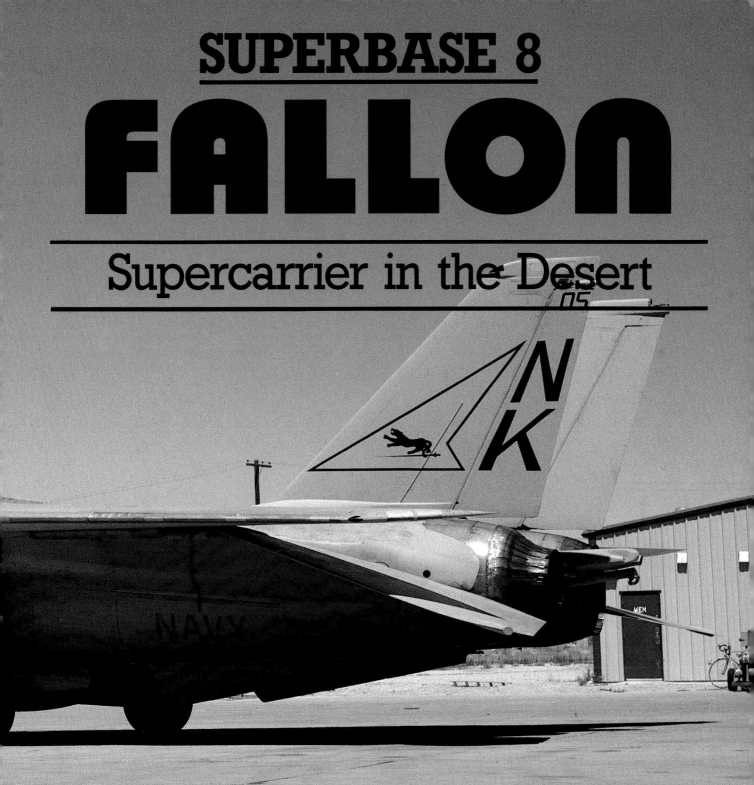

SUPERBASE 8
FALLON
Supercarrier in the Desert

Tony Holmes

Many people have helped the author during the compilation of this book but in particular I would like to thank Commander Olin Briggs, USNR, and his delightful Public Affairs Office staff. Captain Bud Orr and the men at CVW-14 also contributed significantly, as did Captain Bob Brodsky and his XO at NSWC, Commander Rod Maskew. Thanks also to base CO, Captain Wendell Alcorn and VFA-127 boss, Commander Ridge 'Junkyard' Corbin. Finally, a big thank you to Rear Admiral Jeremy 'Bear' Taylor and Captain Ross Underhill (retired) for their organizational help and their ability to 'smooth out' some of the technical hiccups encountered on the way.

Published in 1989 by Osprey Publishing Limited
59 Grosvenor Street, London W1X 9DA

© Tony Holmes 1989

British Library Cataloguing in Publication Data
Holmes, Tony
  Fallon
  1. Nevada. Fallon. Air bases. Fallon Naval Air Station
  I. Title
  358.4'17'0979352

ISBN 0-85045-929-X

Front cover NAS Fallon is all about the tactical training of pilots and aircrews, putting the 'sharp edge' back on the air wing. One of the vital tools in this training process is the venerable A-4F Skyhawk. Although the Skyhawk was designed as a light attack aircraft over 30 years ago, the US Navy has thoroughly exploited the agility of Ed Heinemann's classic over the past two decades. VFA-127 'Cylons', based at Fallon, are masters at wringing out every last drop of ACM manoeuvrability from the Skyhawk

Back cover A veritable army of 'wooden' weapons are dispersed all over the ranges at Fallon, thus heightening the realism of the missions flown there

Title pages Soon to be towed into the maintenance hangar for some routine engine work, this F-14A of VF-21 'Freelancers' basks in the warm Nevada sunshine. Tomcat '207' is a particularly rare machine in VF-21, as it wears the only low-vis paint scheme in the squadron

Right Many A-4 Skyhawks have ended their flying days at NAS Fallon, usually as decoys on the target range, but this veteran A-4C now resides permanently in a far more distinguished position near the station main gate. Unfortunately no US Navy adversary squadrons ever flew the 'C' model Skyhawk. At least the colour scheme is authentic!

For Lieutenant Mark 'Doppler' Lange. Your loss was not in vain

Introduction

Many miles separate the war ravaged city of Beirut from NAS Fallon in Nevada. However, events in the skies over the Lebenese capital half a decade ago unwittingly ensured that the sleepy little air station would assume a place of prominence in US naval aviation in the ensuing years.

On 4 December 1983, a series of events involving the American presence in the Lebanon came to a head. A strike force consisting of A-6 Intruders and A-7 Corsairs from USS *Independence* (CV-62), and Intruders from USS *John F Kennedy* (CV-67), was sent in to bomb a Syrian ammunition dump, a radar antenna dish, and surface-to-air missile (SAM) sites. Political and strategic considerations resulted in the strike being ineffectual with two aircraft lost and a pilot killed.

Almost immediately, changes were made in the training syllabus for strike leaders, and the air wing in general. The most important of these changes was the establishment of the Naval Strike Weapons Center (NSWC) at NAS Fallon in October 1984. Modelled on the highly successful Naval Fighter Weapons School (NFWS), 'Top Gun', at NAS Miramar, the Strike Center has had a profound effect on NAS Fallon, nicknamed 'the biggest little air station in the world'.

Situated at 3000 feet above sea-level alongside the impressive Sierra Nevada mountain range, Fallon has always been associated with the training of aviators. Hastily constructed in 1942, Fallon was one of five bases from which the potential 'air war over San Francisco' was to have been fought when a Japanese assault on the Californian coast seemed imminent. Controlled by the US Army Air Corps, the base eventually became the final stop for bomber crews completing their training before being posted to Europe or the Pacific.

Fallon became a Navy possession in 1944 and over the past 45 years virtually all 'tailhookers' have peppered the high desert with live ordnance at some time in their career. During the Vietnam conflict air wings worked up thoroughly at the air station just prior to departing for the Tonkin Gulf.

Blessed with fine weather for 361 days a year on average, Fallon is the perfect spot for strike training. Almost $200 million will have been spent on improving the ranges and establishing the NWSC by the end of the 1980s. A Tactical Air Combat Training System (TACTS), similar to the one at Nellis Air Force Base, gives flying at NAS Fallon a realism that is unsurpassed anywhere in the world.

On average 11 air wings visit Fallon in a year, a figure which underlines the importance of the air station in modern US Naval carrier operations. Perhaps the ultimate accolade should come from a seasoned 'tailhooker' who recently passed through 'the biggest little air station' for the umpteenth time.

'When we are here, it is *the* most exciting flying we do, and *the* most challenging'. *Captain Bud Orr, Commander Air Group (CAG), Carrier Air Wing 14*

Contents

Right Operating alongside Skyhawks and F-5E Tiger IIs, VFA-127 'Cylons' also employs a number of F-5Fs in the adversary role. The twin seat Tiger II is as combat capable as its single seat brother, and like the Navy F-5Es, no radar is mounted in the aircraft's nose

F-5 Tiger II

Below Based at Fallon since October 1987, VFA-127 formerly called Naval Air Station Lemoore, in California, home. The 'Cylons' received their F-5s from the Naval Fighter Weapons School and VF-45 when both of these units traded up to the potent F-16N in 1987. VFA-127 also took delivery of eight former USAF 527th TFTS F-5s last year from RAF Alconbury. The F-5 is a basic fighter when compared to its adversaries at NAS Fallon, the F-14 and the F-18. However, the élite band of 18 pilots assigned to VFA-127 turn the small Northrop fighter into a deadly opponent, more than a match for the fleet 'heavyweights'

Left Several T-38 Talons are also flown by VFA-127 in the adversary role. These aircraft, like the F-5s, are ex-'Top Gun' machines. The Talon was the forerunner of the highly successful F-5 series of fighters and was privately developed by Northrop under the designation N-156T. Although the Talon was designed in the 1950s it still performs admirably in the blue skies over Fallon

9

Above US Navy adversary squadrons and their USAF counterparts have
always been known for the lavish paint schemes which adorn their aircraft,
and VFA-127 are no exception. Although two gun barrels protrude from the
nose of the F-5F, the aircraft has only one M-39 cannon fitted. The right
barrel acts as a cooling scoop for avionics mounted in the nose

Right above The F-5Fs flown by the Navy differ in several respects from
their USAF brothers. The Air Force has never operated the two seater as an
aggressor aircraft, using them to train foreign pilots only. They also have
radar fitted which leads to the third difference between navalized and Air
Force F-5Fs. To provide the proper balance for the aircraft after the longer
nose and extra cockpit had been added, a 300 pound weight had to be
bolted on between the engines beneath the aircraft. As mentioned before,
the Navy F-5F has no radar and this lack of extra weight in the nose means
the aircraft can dispense with the weight

Right below Like several other operators of the F-5, VFA-127 has recently
experienced some problems with wing over-stressing on their aircraft.
This has resulted in the grounding of their machines and the dismantling of
the wing area from the fuselage. The wing is then X-rayed for faults and re-
stressed if necessary. The overall wing area on the F-5E is quite small and
this detracts from its air combat manoeuvrability as the CO of VFA-127,
Commander Ridge 'Junkyard' Corbin, explains. 'The F-5 bleeds off speed
and energy terribly during a big "bat turn" but in a straight line it has the
speed to track down an F-18.' This particular F-5E is temporarily grounded,
hence the tarpaulins over the cannon barrels, canopy, and engine exhausts

The twin engine arrangement in the T-38A is one of the neatest and most compact powerplant packages ever designed. The General Electric J85-GE-5 engine is a development of the YJ85-GE-1 used to power the USAF's Hound Dog missile in the 1950s. This Talon wears a two-tone grey scheme which is one of the most effective worn by adversary aircraft

QT-38 Talon

Formerly based at the Naval Weapons Center (NWC) at China Lake in California, this QT-38A was acquired by VFA-127 when it became redundant to the Center's needs. Flown for a short time by the squadron XO, the Talon was found to be riddled throughout with corrosion. Permanently grounded as a result, Commander Corbin was desperately trying to get it struck off the squadron books at the time of the author's visit

F-16N Falcon

Left The ultimate adversary. Although based at NAS Miramar in southern California, VF-126 'Bandits' and the Naval Fighter Weapons School usually take it in turns to temporarily send a quartet of F-16Ns to Fallon to help VFA-127 with the ACM training of the deployed air wing. Representing a fourth generation adversary like the MiG-29 or the Mirage 2000, the 'nautical' Falcon has slotted into the Navy's ACM training programme superbly. This F-16N belongs to VF-126 and is being pre-flighted by the civilian groundcrew from General Dynamics just prior to departing on an F-16 and A-4 versus an F-18 mission

Inset The F-16 is not a big aircraft, but then neither is this sailor from VF-126! Plugged into the pilot's intercom, she informs him that the tailerons, flaps, slats, and rudder are all performing as they should when he operates them from within the cockpit. Mounted on the wingtip pylon above her head is a dummy AIM-9L Sidewinder missile

Above The view from the cockpit in the F-16 is unsurpassed by any of its contemporaries. This important factor, combined with the aircraft's excellent thrust to weight ratio and remarkable agility, makes the Falcon virtually unbeatable in ACM

Right Powered by a single General Electric F110-GE-100 turbofan, similar to that which is being installed in the F-14A Plus and the F-14D, the F-16N is the 'hot rod' of the Falcon family. Using only a basic radar and dispensing with the M61A-1 rotary cannon, the F-16N is a very lightweight fighter. The VF-126 badge on the tail combines a Soviet star with a front-on view of the F-16. Previously the small profile of the A-4 adorned the red star

Left Seen here at NAS Miramar, the 'Top Gun' school regularly sends its aircraft to Fallon depending on its own operational requirements. This TF-16N is one of a pair in the squadron. The distinctive 'Top Gun' badge is clearly visible on the tail of the aircraft

Above This impressive line-up of VF-126 Falcons has an interloper within their midst. The fifth aircraft in the stack belongs to the Weapons School. The US Navy operates 22 F-16Ns and four TF-16s which are split between the east and west coast air stations. Twelve are based at NAS Key West in Florida with VF-45, the 'Top Gun' school has 12, and VF-126 has six aircraft on strength

A-4F 'Super Fox'

Numerically the most important aircraft operated by VFA-127 is the A-4 Skyhawk, over a dozen single and two seat A-4s are assigned to the squadron. Only two of these aircraft are 'Super Fox' versions of the Skyhawk though, this vividly coloured machine being one of them. The 'Super Fox' A-4 has an uprated Pratt & Whitney P-8 engine installed which gives 'Heinemann's hot rod' an even hotter performance. With a one-to-one thrust to weight ratio the aircraft can in fact out-climb an F-18, and pull five to six G without losing airspeed. All this is good news for adversary pilot and bad news for their opponents! Eventually all the squadron A-4Fs will be re-engined

Above The TA-4J is a unique machine in that it can perform the role of an *ab initio* mount just as well as it fulfils the position of an adversary aircraft. VFA-127 often fly the TA-4 with the back seat occupied as all their aviators must undergo rigorous training within the squadron before they can eventually call themselves adversary pilots

Right The large one-piece canopy on the TA-4J is heavily framed and restricts the pilot's field of view, but generally speaking his rearward vision is better than in the single seat A-4F

Left The A-4F is an old machine, but put into the hands of an experienced pilot it will run rings around anyone who is stupid enough to try and turn with it, or attempt to engage in ACM at a speed lower than 500 knots. Wearing a rather worn desert scheme, this particular A-4 has a 'borrowed' leading-edge slat affixed to its port wing

Above No prizes for guessing to which squadron this 'bone dome' belongs

Far left Before each mission the pilot performs the age-old ritual of the aviator—the pre-flight walkaround. Once he has looked over the aircraft from the ground he climbs onto his mount and runs through a memorized list of upper airframe checks. Here he thoroughly inspects the engine fuel system panel.

Left The pilot takes a quick look at the UHF aerial and then glances across the ramp at his opposition, a row of F-18s parked only a few feet away

Right The A-4 cockpit has never been known for its spaciousness but this veteran pilot has performed the delicate routine of fitting into the Skyhawk on more than one occasion. Below him his Navy plane captain prepares to pull away the crew ladder. Navy groundcrew are a rarity at NAS Fallon as civilian personnel perform most of the on and off ramp duties. VFA-127 alone has over 120 Lockheed employees assigned to it

Far right The archetypal gunfighter. A century ago Fallon was a typical 'wild west' town and shoot-outs were a common everyday occurrence. Nothing much has changed over the past 100 years

Left Because of the extreme heat at Fallon squadron members often taxi out with their canopies still open. Waiting in the queue to take off, this particular pilot quickly checks the split trailing-edge flaps on his A-4F

Above Over the years adversary units have tried to make the TA-4 look a little bit more like the aircraft it is supposed to simulate, the MiG-17. This is VFA-127's attempt. Fortunately the beautiful lines of the Skyhawk still show through

Left A shortage of spares for the venerable Skyhawk occasionally leads to the grounding of some 'Cylons' aircraft. 'Because the aircraft is not a top-level, high profile fighter the emphasis placed on it at a spares level leaves a lot to be desired. We have problems getting the parts we need to keep the aircraft operational as a result. The replacement of leading-edge slats is a recurrent problem because the strain we place on them during ACM is far more than was ever expected when the A-4 was designed. The parts replacement is not really geared for it. Slat rails, nuts, bolts, and other assorted gear which goes into replacing these parts is always in short supply', explained Commander Corbin. This particular TA-4 is missing its leading-edge slats

Above Another two seat Skyhawk grounded and sealed up against the elements. About 555 TA-4s were built by McDonnell Douglas between 1965 and 1978. Although powered by the modest P-6 version of the trusty Pratt & Whitney J52, the TA-4 still holds its own when flown skilfully. 'Although the TA-4 has many limitations, in the role that we perform, purely day VFR (visual flight rules) ACM, it is an excellent mount. Its underpowered, but flown by a competent pilot who can exploit the agility of the airframe, it can hold its own with any fighter. We went on a deployment to the USAF F-16 training wing earlier this year (1988) and easily held our own, surprising many of our hosts. They presented us with a plaque at the end of the Det which perfectly summed up their feelings towards us. The inscription read 'Its the MAN in the jet', said Commander Corbin rather proudly

Left A vastly experienced aviator is the best way to describe the head 'Cylon'. Commander Corbin first flew A-7As and Bs with VA-87 'Golden Warriors' on board the USS *Franklin D Roosevelt* (CVA-42) in 1971, taking part in two Mediterranean cruises during his time with the unit. He was then posted to NAS Meridian, Mississippi, as a flight instructor on TA-4s in 1975. Corbin's next assignment was something quite different for US Navy pilots. He was transferred on an exchange programme to the Royal Australian Navy's Fleet Air Arm and assigned to VC-724 flying A-4Gs. After two years he returned to NAS Cecil Field in Florida and transitioned onto the A-7E. Corbin was then sent to VA-82 'Marauders' onboard the USS *Nimitz* (CVN-68). He stayed with the squadron for a record 37 months before being posted to an Army Staff College for a year. He joined VA-127, as it was designated before the arrival of the F-5s and the move to Fallon in May 1986, as XO. 'Junkyard' Corbin assumed command of the squadron in November 1987. 'I've achieved what must be every aviator's dream, having been able to fly for 19 out of the 20 years I've been in the Navy'

Above A rather smart looking A-4F sits out on the ramp. It usually takes a newly arrived pilot at VFA-127 from four months to a year to become a fully fledged AP (Adversary Pilot) from being a PUT (Pilot Under Training). The next stage is an IP (Instructor Pilot) and this can take many months as the pilot takes on fully qualified instructors within the squadron in ACM. Equally as important as the potential instructor's flying skill is his ability to debrief the opposing pilot after the mission has been concluded

Navy Reserve A-4 Skyhawks

Another élite squadron in the US Navy is VFC-13 'Saints', one of two full-time reserve adversary units. Based at Miramar, where they traditionally provide more than 50 per cent of the adversary sorties for fighter squadrons at the air station, VFC-13 regularly send Skyhawks to Fallon. This A-4F has an ECM fin tip antenna housing fitted, a modification not seen on VFA-127 aircraft

Opposite above Carrying a dayglo Aircraft Instrumentation Systems (AIS) pod, alternatively known as an Air Combat Manoeuvring (ACMI) pod, on the inner wing pylon, a TA-4J is readied for the first flight of the morning. This particular aircraft still wears the old style tail code and VC-13 unit designation. The 'Saints' recently underwent a squadron redesignation from a fleet composite unit to a fighter composite unit, a title which better describes their role

Opposite below With its all-moving tailplane angled steeply, airbrakes deployed, trailing edge flaps split, and tailhook lowered, the reserve pilot of this TA-4 runs through the pre-flight checks on his aircraft. A posting to VFC-13 is a most sought after position as the pilots are permanently shore based and essentially part-time naval aviators, although they usually fly five days a week! Needless to say, to be a 'Saint' adversary you have to be one of the best

Above Whenever an aircraft takes off at Fallon it usually has an AIS/ACI pod mounted under the wing. These pods fit onto the AIM-9 launch rails and transmit data back to the Tactical Air Combat Training System (TACTS) computer which converts the information into imagery on two large screens in the TACTS centre. Altitude, speed, and distance from other aircraft are all sensed by the pod, as well as accurate scoring of engagements

The end of the road

Eventually all combat aircraft reach the end of the line and make their final flight to Davis-Monthan Air Force Base to begin long-term storage. Ultimately they will be struck off charge and sold for scrap to local metal merchants. One A-4 that will never bask in the Arizona sunshine is this battered C model which once served onboard the USS *John F Kennedy* (CV-67). The remains of this disembowelled Skyhawk are scattered over a wide area away from the busy Fallon ramps

The Mighty Tomcat

Left At the opposite end of the fighter spectrum from the diminutive A-4 Skyhawk is the large and powerful F-14 Tomcat, the US Navy's main air superiority fighter. Carrier Air Wing (CVW) 14, just like most other air wings, has two Tomcat squadrons assigned to it, VF-21 'Freelancers' and VF-154 'Black Knights'. Unlike those of other air wings, CVW-14's Tomcats are arguably the most colourful in the entire Navy. This VF-21 machine looks resplendent as it taxies out bathed in the early morning sun

Below The 'Freelancers' were formed at Alameda in California on 1 July 1959 when VF-64 was redesignated during a Navy clean-up of carrier air groups (CVGs). Equipped with the McDonnell F3H-2 Demon, the squadron was assigned to CVG-2 and embarked on the USS *Midway* (CVA-41). After three cruises with the rather lacklustre Demon the squadron was shifted to Miramar and began the conversion onto the F-4B Phantom II. In March 1965 the squadron sailed on their first combat cruise to Vietnam, a route they would traverse a further five times over the following eight years. During this inaugural cruise VF-21 shot down two MiG-17s, the first US Navy kills of the war, and the only victories achieved by the 'Freelancers' in the conflict. The squadron also embarked on the USS *Coral Sea* (CVA-43) and the USS *Ranger* (CVA-61) during their wartime cruises. The 'Freelancers' re-equipped with the F-4J in 1968 and continued to fly this model until December 1979. Along with sister squadron VF-154, VF-21 was introduced to

the F-4S, the ultimate Navy Phantom II, soon after relinquishing the last of their rather tired J models. Unfortunately the over-the-ramp speed of the F-4S was deemed to be too fast for VF-21's 'new' carrier, the small USS *Coral Sea*, and they had to trade their Phantoms with VF-301 and VF-302, the Pacific Fleet's reserve fighter units. Eventually in November 1983, along with VF-154, the 'Freelancers' finally said goodbye to their venerable F-4Ns, thus making these two squadrons the last US-based units to fly the Navy F-4 in frontline service. The age of the Tomcat was soon to begin

Right Soon to be airborne and tackling A-4s and F-16s, a row of F-14s from VF-21 sit quietly whilst their crews go through the final briefings before the mission

Below Offering a complete contrast to other aircraft in the squadron, Tomcat '205' wears a full low-visibility scheme, although the pair of external tanks mounted underneath the F-14 are obviously borrowed from a glossy machine. The mobile gantry alongside the aircraft's tail was used by a squadron maintenance man to apply the unit markings to the freshly painted tail fin

Left Crewed-up and ready to go, a VF-154 pilot sweeps the wings out on his big Grumman fighter. This check is always performed just before taxiing out. The heavy weathering around the engine intake is rather unusual

Below The plane captain hand-cranks the boarding ladder down into place in preparation for the arrival of the crew. The myriad of warning and rescue markings show out distinctively on this aircraft. These markings, along with the full size 'star and bar', are rather more subdued on the low-vis machines

Inset While his radar intercept officer (RIO) begins the pre-flight check around the all-moving tailplane, the pilot juggles around with his survival vest which straps on over his flight suit

Right A formidable line-up of 'Black Knights'. The squadron can trace its origins back to 1953 when VF-837, a reserve unit, was redesignated VF-154 at Moffett Field in California. Assigned to Carrier Air Group 15 aboard the USS *Yorktown* (CVA-10), the 'Black Knights' flew the Grumman F9F-5 Panther until converting onto the North American FJ-3 Fury in 1955 and joining the USS *Wasp* (CVA-18). IN 1957 VF-154 became the first operational Pacific Fleet squadron to receive the F8U-1 Crusader, sailing on a WestPac cruise in February 1958 as part of CVG-15 on the USS *Hancock* (CVA-19). Various models of Crusader were flown by VF-154 over the next seven years on a handful of operational deployments, including a combat cruise to Vietnam on board the USS *Coral Sea* in 1964/65. The first half of 1966 was spent transitioning onto the F-4B at Miramar, joining CVW-2 for another combat cruise in late July, once again on the *Coral Sea*. Another five cruises to Vietnam lay ahead for the 'Black Knights' but on board the USS *Ranger*. The squadron's major post-war activities mirror those of its sister unit VF-21 in almost every respect. One difference between the two squadrons however, is that VF-154 is the Tactical Air Reconnaissance Pod System (TARPS) unit in CVW-14. Three TARPS configured F-14s are usually operated by the squadron

Above left G-suits are not the most comfortable of things at the best of times, just ask this 'Black Knight'. Behind his right shoulder is an AIS/ACMI pod

Above right Constrained firmly within his G-suit, the RIO delicately climbs aboard his 'trusty steed'. Even with the ladder, fold-out steps, and 'kick-in' boarding slots to help the crew, getting into the F-14 wearing all the extraneous gear associated with the modern aviator is still an acrobatic feat

Right The black and scarlet colours worn on the twin tails of the F-14 are similar in style to those which adorned the various models of Phantom II that the 'Black Knights' flew in the 1960s and 70s. The wings on this Tomcat are in the over-sweep position

Above RIOs, as well as pilots, can command frontline fighter squadrons in the US Navy. Proving just that, Commander Jim 'Meatball' Santangelo takes his place in the back seat of his F-14. Santangelo has been 'head knight' of VF-154 since March 1988

Right Afterburner is lighted and the brakes released. In a matter of seconds this VF-154 Tomcat will be roaring down Fallon's 14,000 foot runway. The black top at the air station is the longest west of the Mississippi. An 11,000 foot runway is currently being built parallel to the existing one to allow the air station to remain open all year

The 'Black Knight Mobile'

The 'official' staff car of VF-154 is a rather large and extremely ugly Plymouth Fury. Fully marked up in squadron colours, the 'Yank tank' can carry a 'war load' of over 20 cases of beer, very useful for long range sorties

Abused Feline

Left In mid-1987 CVW-6 came to Fallon for work-ups just prior to deploying on board the USS *Forrestal* (CV-59) for the first time. One of the squadrons which belonged to the air wing was VF-31 'Tomcatters', a very distinguished unit. Unfortunately for the squadron one of their F-14s was accidentally rammed by a bowser truck while it was parked on the flightline. The truck hit the Tomcat in the wing glove area and inflicted considerable damage on the aircraft. The bowser truck was written off and its driver seriously injured. Over a year later repairs had almost been completely effected on the relatively new F-14 and it was expected to rejoin VF-31 soon after the author saw it at Fallon

Below The 'Tomcatters' are the second oldest US Navy fighter squadron, receiving the designation VF-31 in August 1948 when VF-3A was re-numbered. Over the years the squadron has flown the F8F Bearcat, F9F-2 Panther, F2H-2 Banshee, F3H-2 Demon, and the F-4 Phantom II. The 'Tomcatters' even undertook a single Vietnam combat cruise in 1972/73, the highlight of the 10 month deployment being the downing of a MiG-21 on 21 June 1972. In August 1980 the squadron began the transition onto the F-14 at NAS Oceana in Florida, VF-31's home since 1965. The black radome and scarlet tail are distinguishing features of VF-31

Inset The 'Felix the Cat' emblem has been worn by many classic Navy fighters over the years, originating in the 1930s on early Boeing biplanes. 'Felix' has weathered the test of time well and VF-31 continues to build on a fine naval tradition

The sting of the Hornet

Below CVW-14 is unique amongst west coast air wings. As it is the only frontline group which includes two squadrons of F-18s within its complement of aircraft. These F-18s belong to VFA-113 'Stingers', the first operational Navy unit to transition onto the Hornet in April 1983 from the A-7E Corsair

Right 'Let it all hang out.' The rudders are angled inwards, the large airbrake is fully deployed, the single slotted Fowler-type flaps are in the extended position, the tailhook is down, and the refuelling probe is out. Once the pilot is satisfied all the above mentioned items are operating just as McDonnell Douglas intended them to he will tidy up the appearance of his Hornet and signal that 'Stinger 305' is ready to taxi out

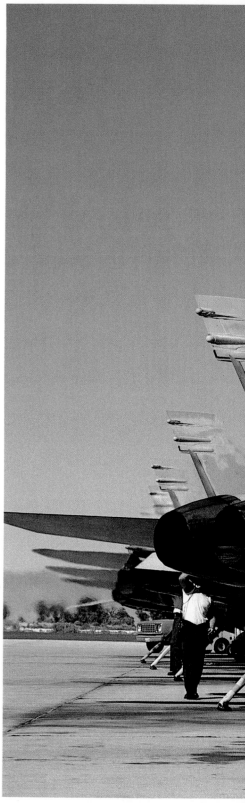

Opposite above 'Stinger 305' rolls out towards the main taxi ramp. The ensuing mission will involve four VFA-113 Hornets pitted against four VFA-127 Skyhawks and a pair of VF-126 F-16Ns. VFA-25 and VFA-113 seem to favour carrying a single tank on each inner wing pylon, whereas most other F-18 units usually mount a single 330 US gallon tank on the centre pylon. Whatever the mix, the Hornet's rather short range is the major 'Achilles' heel' of the aircraft

Opposite below VFA-113 were a very colourful squadron ten years ago when they were equipped with A-7E Corsairs. Just over 20 years ago the 'Stingers' were flying the diminutive A-4C Skyhawk over the jungles of Vietnam. Nowadays the squadron is equipped with a mixture of BuNo Block 17 and 18 A model Hornets

Above Bombed up and ready to taxi away from the high-explosive loading pad, the pilot waits for his ground crewman to finish his final check before departing. The small rectangular fillet attached to the wing shoulder is a relatively new modification being retrofitted to F-18s to alter the airflow around the twin tails and reduce strain on these areas. Over-stressing of the tail units has been another problem which has consistently plagued the Hornet

Left The second unit in CVW-14 equipped with the F-18 is VFA-25 'Fist of the Fleet.' The squadron took delivery of its first Hornet on 11 November 1983, and 16 months later participated in the aircraft's first operational cruise, along with VFA-113, when the USS *Constellation* (CV-64) departed on a WestPac deployment in February 1985. The twin variable nozzles of the General Electric F404 turbofans are quite small in diameter. A spate of unexplained engine fires has plagued both Navy and Marine Corps Hornets over the past 18 months and a vast sum of money has been spent trying to find a solution. As one pilot put it 'the engine was too good to be true. So much thrust in so small a package. The trade-off was reliability

Above Whereas once a posting to the fighter community was considered to be the plum job, young pilots now prefer to head for light attack country. This lieutenant from VFA-25 is just one of many pilots who are experiencing their first taste of flying at NAS Fallon

A-6E TRAM Intruder

Left Fallon is all about putting bombs on targets accurately, and one of the best aircraft in the business for doing just that is the Intruder. CVW-14's A-6 squadron is VA-196 'Main Battery', based at NAS Whidbey Island in Washington state. During the air wing's three week deployment to Fallon the ten or twelve A-6E TRAM aircraft which form the offensive part of the attack squadron are usually parked on the high-explosive ramp. This saves turn-around time between sorties

Below The 'Main Battery' is an ex-Skyraider squadron, having flown the venerable 'Spad' during the Vietnam War. Surprisingly the A-6 is not a good visual bombing platform, its forte being radar guided low-level penetration attacks. The Intruder's replacement, the almost physically identical A-6F, has been put on ice for the moment to try and save funding for the Advanced Tactical Aircraft (ATA), the proposed 'wonder weapon' for the Navy of the 1990s

Above The high-explosive ramp at Fallon is quite a large area close to the armaments depot. A modern facility, the bombing up pan can handle a large number of aircraft at the one time. The two 'partners in strike' of CVW-14, the F-18 Hornet and the A-6E TRAM Intruder, were the armourers' main customers during the wing's 18 day stay. This particular Intruder, BuNo 160427, is a relatively new aircraft compared to some still knocking around in frontline service

Right The armourers have finished work on this Intruder and now it sits awaiting the pilot and bombadier/navigator. The engine covers are hinged open and the external starter hoses are plugged in. The A-6 is a physically intimidating machine, the true workhorse of the air wing. Carrying a comparatively small bomb load, by its standards, of only six retarded Mk 82 500 pounders, this VA-196 belongs to the squadron CO

Right With the temperature hovering around 100 °F any bit of shade is occupied with relish, just ask these rather warm 'ordies' as they sit beneath the tailplane of CAG's A-6. The aircraft has the ventral equipment bay, or simply the 'birdcage', lowered to allow the squadron maintenance men to check the Intruder's electronics. This particular A-6 started life over 20 years ago as an A model, before being updated into its present configuration in the early 1980s

Above Early morning activity on the ramp at Fallon. The only difference between this 'mule' and those seen scooting around on the decks of carriers is that this particular one has no jet engine starter mounted on the back. The hangars in the distance belong to VFA-127 and are used periodically by dets from VFA-106 and 125, the east and west coast F-18 training squadrons

Inset Because Fallon is the major live weapons range for the US Navy it is logical that ordnance technicians, or 'red shirts', should undertake their initial training at the air station. 'Ordies' usually spend 18 months at Fallon learning how to assemble bombs, fuse them safely, and load them correctly. This particular armourer is not part of the training course however, the rather battered VA-196 sticker on his cranial indicating that he is in fact a 'Main Battery' man

Right Clearly visible in this view of the Intruder is the target recognition attack multisensor (TRAM) pod. The first TRAM equipped squadron to operate from a carrier deck was VA-165 'Boomers' when they deployed onboard the USS *Constellation* in 1977. The small ball turret beneath the radome is partly retractable and contains both forward looking infra-red radar (FLIR) and laser sensors. This allows the crew to watch real-time television imagery of non-visual, or radar targets, and further enhances the Intruder's already formidable all-weather bombing capability

Refuellers

Below Leaving us in no doubt that this is indeed a KA-6D, every possible hardpoint on the aircraft has a large external fuel tank attached to it. Typically, Intruder squadrons have four KA-6Ds on strength and these vital aircraft usually perform the bulk of refuelling duties for the air wing. VA-196 was soon to be joined by VS-37 'Sawbucks' in the tanker role as the Viking squadron was expecting to take charge of one of the first plumbed KS-3As during the Fallon deployment

Above 'Starting number two.' This signal by the pilot informs the attending ground crew that he is spooling up the second Pratt & Whitney J52-P-8A turbojet engine, mounted almost directly beneath him

Right The Navy at one stage low-vised some of their Intruder tankers but quickly reverted back to full colours when other pilots indicated that they were having trouble spotting the aircraft, and judging distances between probe and drogue when close up to the KA-6. The squadron's stock of external tanks are low-vis however

Squadron colours are clearly in evidence on the tail of this KA-6D. Attack squadrons take pride in the appearance of their tankers, flying monuments to former colourful glory days. The Navy originally had 71 early A-6As converted to KA-6D standard during the early 1970s, fitting the refuelling system in the ventral 'birdcage'. Current Navy plans call for the venerable Intruder tanker to soldier on until at least the year 2000. If this particular machine is still flying then it will be close to 40 years old

EA-6B Prowler

Left Over $100 million worth of high-tech aircraft sit on the ramp in front of CVW-14's temporary maintenance hangar. VAQ-139 'Cougars' are a relatively new EA-6B squadron and like all other Prowler units, call the picturesque air station on Whidbey Island home. The EA-6B has been produced in no less than five different variants, although the basic outward appearance of the aircraft has remained essentially unchanged. Prowler '605' is one of 45 ICAP 1 (improved capability) aircraft built, and in all probability has been updated to ICAP 2 standard. The differences between these aircraft basically centre around improved computer and electronic warfare capabilities

Inset When viewed from the front the Prowler looks a lot like the aircraft from which it was developed, the A-6 Intruder. To help landing signal officers (LSOs) differentiate between the two aircraft, crosses, or inverted radiation symbols as in this case, are sprayed onto the nose of the Prowler. Mounted on the centreline pylon is one of the EA-6B's main offensive weapons, the AN/ALQ-99E integrally-powered 'smart' jamming pod

Left A Prowler squadron usually operates four aircraft, the smallest unit in the air wing along with the Hawkeye squadron. However, the offensive capability of the air wing depends heavily on the tactical deployment of those four Prowlers. Effective ECM techniques are thoroughly tested at Fallon on the specially built electronic warfare range

Above An effective use of shade. Having finished the briefing for the return flight to NAS Whidbey Island, the crew from Prowler '909' suit up before conducting the pre-flight

Left Partnering Prowler '909' on its brief cross-country foray was Prowler '908'. Both aircraft belonged to VAQ-129 'Vikings', the EA-6B fleet readiness squadron, but were crewed, rather unusually, by members of VAQ-136 'Gauntlets', CVW-5's resident Prowler unit which is forward deployed to NAS Atsugi in Japan

Above left Only a member of the Prowler community could wear a 'bone dome' like this

Above right 'Ekmo 3' sorts out his office before climbing in. The role of this particular electronic countermeasures officer (ECMO), to give him his proper title, is to operate the Sanders Associates AN/ALQ-92 communications jamming system. The weapon's effectiveness was shown in 1986 when it was used extensively by the US Sixth Fleet, during Operations Prairie Fire and El Dorado Canyon, to completely obliterate all Libyan military communications traffic

E-2C Hawkeye

The mobile nerve centre of the air wing, the E-2C Hawkeye is vital for effective co-ordination of aircraft over the strike area. Flying many hours when deployed at sea, the aircraft and crews of the VAW squadrons spend a considerable period of their time at Fallon airborne as well. VAW-113 are the unit attached to CVW-14, and the aircraft they took to Fallon had only recently been obtained from VAW-117, a sister squadron based at NAS Miramar

Viking Strike

Left You may wonder what a dedicated anti-submarine warfare aircraft like the S-3A Viking does during the air wing's three weeks at Fallon, an air station which is most definitely 'waterless'. Well, the armourers mount triple ejector racks (TERs) on the single underwing hardpoints and the S-3 boys go out and cause havoc on the weapons range. This particular Viking from VS-37 'Sawbucks' has just returned from a sortie with a Mk 82 bomb stuck up on one of its TERs. This tends to raise the anxiety level of the crew slightly until the bomb is made safe by a team of armourers specially trained to deal with these problems

Below The *shade* of things to come. Most S-3 squadrons now have one or two of their aircraft sprayed up in low-vis colours. The 'Sawbucks' are based at NAS North Island in San Diego, and like most other ASW squadrons, flew the S-2 Tracker for many years before updating to the 'whispering hoover' in the eary 1970s. The day before this photo was taken Viking '703' had scored the most amazing direct hit on a smoke flare which was marking the 'target' for attacking aircraft on the Bravo 17 range

Above The 'hard grunt' of loading the retarded bomb now over, the armourers tighten up the anti-sway braces and sort out the fuse wiring for the detonator cap which will screw into the O-shaped ring at the front of the weapon

Right Fully bombed up and ready to go. The Viking was never designed to be a dive bomber and as a result no sophisticated weapons delivery radar is fitted. The crew rely on the 'Mark One Eyeball' and a trusty grease pencil line strategically placed on the windscreen. This unlikely combination, together with the S-3's excellent flying characteristics, make the Viking 'strike team' a formidable force

The ramp

When the air wing's in town the ramp at Fallon becomes a very lively place. In the foreground is the combined VFA-127/Air Wing 14 ramp, and in the distance is the high-explosive loading pad. A total of 40 aircraft are present in this view taken from the NAS Fallon control tower

Home on the range

Left 'The enemy'. To create as real a scenario as possible for the strike aircraft operating on Bravo 17, the 4th Land Air Missile Squadron (LAMS) of the US Marine Corps deployed to Fallon from Fresno, California. Equipped with the Raytheon HAWK (homing-all-the-way-killer) MIM-23 surface-to-air missile, 'Charlie' battery set up shop on a flat plain overlooking the bomb drop area on the range. In the foreground is the tracker/illuminator radar, and behind it an empty three-round missile launcher. Alongside 'Charlie' battery was a mock army camp, a challenging target for the F-18s and A-6s of CVW-14. The HAWK system is also used by the Iranian Army, amongst other users, so the tactics formulated by the air wing to counter the effectiveness of the SAM could possibly save lives in the future

Below A total of 30 marines man this particular battery, an unenviable task in the scorching heat of the Nevada desert. During the brief time the author spent with 'Charlie' battery 32 strikes were made against imaginary targets on Bravo 17. These attacks were flown by a mixed force of F-18s, S-3s, A-6s, and EA-6s, and the men from the 4th LAMS theoretically knocked down 32 aircraft! One wonders what that figure would have looked like if a couple of 'imaginary' AGM-88 HARMs (high-velocity anti-radiation missiles) had been fired in the direction of 'Charlie' battery before the strikes started?

Left Leased from the US Army and
used extensively by the Naval Strike
Weapons Center (NSWC) is the
M-60 based Sergeant Yorke air
defence tracking tank. 'The Army
built about 100 of these tanks but
there were allegations of cost
overruns and doubts cast as to
whether it could perform the job it
was designed for so the project was
stopped. We have been able to
lease several from the Army and we
use them extensively out on the
ranges. They have laser optical
trackers and finders, acquisition
radar, and the finest electro-optical
system I've ever seen. It is armed
with a twin 40 mm gun and also
boasts a low-light TV camera. We
put a video recorder in the turret,
hook it up to the radar, and then use
the resulting tape as an aid when
debriefing aviators. We can show
them being tracked visually on the
range, or on radar, or on the
electro-optical system.' So says
Captain Bob Brodsky, CO of the
NSWC

Above Affectionately known as the
'checkerboard' or the 'big golf ball',
this building is the electronic brain
of strike warfare at NAS Fallon.
Every move made by aircraft
equipped with an AIS/ACMI pod on

any one of five 'live' ranges is automatically tracked and displayed within this building by the Tactical Air Combat Training System. The five ranges simulate different scenarios likely to be encountered by an air wing. Bravo 16 is south west of the air station and, like the following three ranges, has a TV camera scoring system mounted near the drop point. Bravo 17, east of NAS Fallon, has had a mock army camp, industrial site, powerplant, runway with aircraft (old A-4s), weapons revetments, and dummy missile sites with electronic emitters, all built onto it over the past five years. A no-drop electronic bomb scoring system recently installed combines with the above mentioned features to make this range the busiest of the five. The electronic warfare, or 'Echo Whiskey', range was created during the Vietnam War and has the capability to simulate threats from Soviet SAMs and *Gun Dish* radar. South of the base is Bravo 19, a mountainous area ideal for close air support training, as well as simulated truck convoy strikes. The final range is Bravo 20, nicknamed 'Lone Rock'. This range has been operational since 1943 and is used for dumping ordnance should a pilot encounter trouble with his aircraft. During 1988 Bravo 20 was closed while it underwent a complete overhaul. All the gadgetry installed on the other ranges was being added to Bravo 20 during the refurbishment to allow it to be compatible with the TACTS system

Inset No question of cost overruns here! This mock SAM launcher is just part of the extensive wooden and plastic army which calls Bravo 17 home

'Now where did I park that bus!' The end of the line for many clapped-out service buses is at Fallon. One of these unlucky vehicles is parked in the middle of the bullseye on Bravo 17 every seven to ten days because they don't usually last much longer than that. Studies have been carried out by the NSWC showing that the accuracy of pilots drops markedly when no bus is present. God help the enemy if they travel to the battlefield in olive drab buses!

SH-3H
Sea King

Left A line-up of 'Eightballers'. HELANTISUBRON (HS) Eight sent three Sea Kings to Fallon as part of the CVW-14 deployment, but like VS-37, not a lot of ASW work was completed! While the squadron was at the air station they concentrated on learning combat SAR (Search and Rescue) techniques developed specially by the NSWC for HS units

Below The Sea King's distinctive hull shaped lower fuselage is clearly visible in this close-up. The lip of the fuselage actually hinges outwards to allow squadron maintainers access to various radar and instrument panel assemblies easily and quickly

Pilot and co-pilot complete final pre-flight checks before taxiing out to the launch ramp. HS-8 removed all the ASW equipment from their Sea Kings and left it behind at NAS North Island, their home base. This gave the 'Eightballers' extended flying time on the range and helped their venerable mounts cope with the 'high and hot' conditions experienced at Fallon

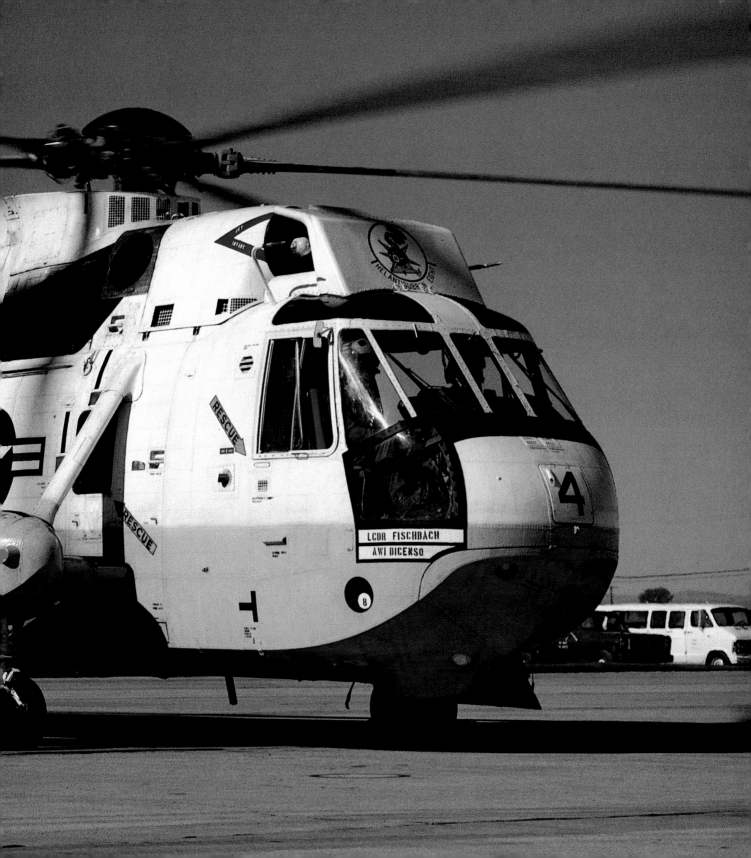

Left Combat SAR has been neglected over the years by the Navy but the NSWC now places a strong emphasis on it. This Sea King is undergoing early morning inspection by its assigned maintainers before the crew arrive to undertake the first combat SAR sortie of the day

Above After the rotor blades are extended from their stowed position they are thoroughly checked by an agile ground crewman. He remains in a stationary position on the opened engine hatch cover while the pilot carefully rotates each of the five blades around to him

Left To avoid extensive dust clouds and foreign object debris (FOD) problems arising from take-off, helicopters usually taxi away from the dispersal area and depart from a small runway built especially for them

Above The helicopter ramp progresses into the Fallon transient ramp the closer it gets to the main runway. Behind this departing HS-8 Sea King can be seen a pair of VAQ-129 Prowlers and a lone USAF OV-10A Bronco

Combat SAR

Regular visitors to Fallon are HC-9, the only dedicated combat SAR unit in the US Navy. HC-9's Sea Kings are often flown by east coast ASW squadrons when their air wings deploy to Fallon. This is because a cross-country haul in a Sea King from NAS Jacksonville, Florida, to NAS Fallon, Nevada, would probably tax the endurance of both helicopter and crew to virtual breaking point!

The HH-3As flown by HC-9 were specially modified D model Sea Kings built
for combat SAR units flying over Vietnam during the late 1960s and early 70s.
The HH-3 has a high-speed refuelling fuel dumping system, bolt on armour,
uprated engines, and twin 7.62 mm Minigun mounts and integral ammunition
belt feeders. The squadron has flown the HH-3 since 1975 and, like other
west coast Sea King squadrons, calls NAS North Island home. All markings on
the HH-3, including warning arrows, are matt black, and the helicopter itself
is painted in a low sheen medium green (Federal Standard 34079)

Also present at Fallon for a week's work-up before deployment was a pair of SH-2F Seasprites which belonged to HSL-35 'Magicians' Det Three. Both the Seasprite and the Sea King have been operated by the US Navy for over 30 years and although the SH-60 Sea Hawk is now well established in rotary ranks, these two venerable types are bound to be serving with frontline units well past the year 2000

Contrasting Seasprites

Left For many years the diminutive Seasprite has worn the traditional glossy engine grey colour scheme reserved exclusively for utility and light ASW helicopters. However, all good things must come to an end. New and reworked Seasprites are filtering through to HSL squadrons wearing the tactical paint scheme (TPS) greys

Below This Seasprite was only delivered to HSL-35 from the Kaman factory in April 1988 and embodies all the current updates developed for the helicopter. The two rather ugly boxes grafted onto the spine of the Seasprite are an integral part of a new electronic warfare system retrofitted to helicopters operating in the Persian Gulf. The ECM 'black boxes' combine with two chaff launcher packs fitted just behind the sonobuoy rack on the opposite side of the Seasprite. The modification didn't work too well initially but HSL-35 were more than pleased with the results of their week's flying on the electronic warfare range

Left Also a brand new Seasprite, this particular machine's only concession to TPS is a pair of low-vis external tanks. The ECM modifications appear to be performed at squadron level because this particular Seasprite had no ALQ boxes mounted on the spine, although the chaff launchers were attached to the fuselage. The prominent servo flaps fitted to the trailing edge of each rotor blade are also quite visible in this view

Above The colourful squadron badge of HSL-35 clearly reflects their nickname. The 'Magicians' have flown the Seasprite since 1973, and are one of eight frontline units equipped with the helicopter. Three Navy Reserve squadrons also operate the SH-2F. A typical squadron complement is 10–12 aircraft from which small shipboard detachments are formed

Another modification recently added to the Seasprite is a FLIR turret which is mounted beneath the nose of the helicopter. Although the actual turret is not fitted to this Seasprite the mounting is visible just beneath the nose modex. HSL-35 Det Three was soon to deploy on a WestPac cruise onboard the USS *Callaghan*, one of four *Kidd* class destroyers in the US Navy. Interestingly, the four *Kidd* class vessels were originally built for the Imperial Iranian Navy but were never delivered following the revolution in that country in 1979. Hence they are nicknamed the '*Ayatollah*' class!

Rescue Huey

Although not a headline grabber, or the ultimate in modern technology, the UH-1N Huey still performs a vital task at NAS Fallon. Two brightly coloured Hueys form the base SAR flight and they are regularly seen out on the various ranges practising their extraction techniques. The flight has no designated number but it does adorn its helicopters with a 'unit' emblem, which also doubles as the helicopter's call sign. Painted on the black anti-glare panel in front of the cockpit is the white outline of a longhorn steer's skull. Immediately above the tilted rotor blade is a tightly banking F-14 returning from an ACM engagement over the desert

NWC Corsairs

Left The Naval Strike Weapons Center operates a mixed bag of aircraft including the A-7E and its two seat derivative, the TA-7C. The NSWC use the aircraft to test different attack profiles on the range, and also to evaluate the TACTS system itself

Below The Navy received a total of 60 TA-7Cs comprising 24 converted A-7Bs and 36 A-7Cs. Between January 1985 and 1987 all surviving TA-7s were re-engined and upgraded by Ling Temco Vought. The rather gutless Pratt & Whitney TF-30 turbofan was swapped for the slightly more powerful Allison TF-41, automatic manoeuvring flaps were installed, new Stencel ejection seats fitted, and an engine monitoring system put in place

Opposite above A rather pale A-7E sits on the NSWC ramp in the mid-afternoon sun. Resting on trolleys beneath the wing hardpoints are an assortment of weapons guidance training devices

Opposite below A combination of man-power and machine-power gets the job done on this Corsair. Although maintained by civilian contractors, the NSWC aircraft still have their underwing stores loaded by naval personnel. The small petrol driven motor connected up to the wing pylon lifts the finless Walleye guided glide bomb from the trolley, via a sturdy chain, to the wing mounting

Above The A-7E is now reaching the end of its service career with the US Navy, most east coast light attack squadrons having already transitioned onto the F-18 Hornet. By the look of this Corsair it too may have reached the end of the operational road also. The NSWC lighting bolt has been painted out on the tail, the Allison TF-41 turbofan has been removed, and the canopy perspex appears to have 'gone west' as well. Pitot tube and antenna covers are in place though, as is the intake tarp, so perhaps Corsair '43' is just taking a well earned rest

Gate guard?

Below Hidden away in an obscure corner of the base, surrounded by old building material and rather ignominiously covered in a canvas tarpaulin, is an ex-VA-204 A-7B Corsair. The story goes that this particular aircraft was flown in from Davis-Monthan AFB several years ago so it could be mounted on a pylon and placed next to the Skyhawk as a gate guard. Priorities changed and the tired old Corsair appears to have been forgotten

Troubled Hornet

Below The NSWC operates two Hornets, and like many other squadrons which fly the aircraft, they spend a lot of their time grounded with powerplant problems. After performing an engine change on this F-18A, civilian technicians run the aircraft up to test if the replacement General Electric F404 turbofans are functioning properly

Strike Intruder

Below The third type regularly flown by the Weapons Center is the A-6 Intruder, several being on strength with the flight. All the pilots and crews assigned to the NSWC are highly experienced in their particular field and have been chosen to work at NAS Fallon because of this

Opposite above The Intruder is a pugnacious looking aircraft, and a potent one. The open hatch on the wing has the ram-air-turbine (RAT) attached to it, a vital piece of machinery should a sudden electrical failure afflict the aircraft. Hanging down beneath the fuselage is the compact equipment 'birdcage'. The large air scoop just forward of the tail was a modification added to the Intruder during the TRAM retrofit. It acts as an air-conditioner for the avionics mounted in the 'birdcage'

Opposite below Intruder '03' is a well travelled aircraft, having joined the Navy as long ago as 1965, one of 64 built by Grumman that year. Almost certainly a Vietnam veteran, this former A-6A has been progressively updated over the ensuing 24 years to its present A-6E TRAM configuration

Low-tech

Left Besides having a complement of almost 30 F-18 Hornets, VFA-125 'Rough Raiders', the west coast replacement air group squadron, also operates a flight of six Cessna 337s as forward air controller (FAC) mounts. These are the only 337s in the US Navy and are ex-civilian aircraft bought up to FAC standard by installing VHF/UHF communications equipment

Below The diminutive little Cessna looks rather out of place in view of its ramp companions. Several 337s are also based at NAS Lemoore, VFA-125's home. These aircraft are flown by F-18 instructors who hold special civil FAA ratings on the 'push-pull' Cessna

Overleaf Doctor Who's Tardis on wheels? No, this quaint little mobile hut is in fact an 'RDO Speedwagon'. The runway duty officer (RDO) uses this wheeled-wonder to communicate with pilots on final approach, just as a landing signals officer (LSO) would do on board an aircraft-carrier. The cool dude sheltering from the sun inside the 'Speedwagon' is Lieutenant Carroll Lefon, an F-18 pilot who doubles as an LSO with VFA-25 'Fist of the Fleet'